WITHDRAWN

NATIVE AMERICAN NATIONS

Comanche

F.A. BIRD

Checkerboard Library

An Imprint of Abdo Publishing
abdobooks.com

ABDOBOOKS.COM

Published by Abdo Publishing, a division of ABDO, PO Box 398166, Minneapolis, Minnesota 55439. Copyright © 2022 by Abdo Consulting Group, Inc. International copyrights reserved in all countries. No part of this book may be reproduced in any form without written permission from the publisher. Checkerboard Library™ is a trademark and logo of Abdo Publishing.

Printed in the United States of America, North Mankato, Minnesota
102021
012022

THIS BOOK CONTAINS RECYCLED MATERIALS

Design and Production: Mighty Media, Inc.
Editor: Liz Salzmann
Cover Photograph: Prisma by Dukas Presseagentur GmbH/Alamy Photo
Interior Photographs: Ad_hominem/Shutterstock Images, p. 7; angie oxley/Shutterstock Images, p. 11; (E385897), Department of Anthropology, Smithsonian Institution, p. 15; Gerardo Bello/AP Images, p. 29; JasonOndreicka/iStockphoto, p. 21; Library of Congress, p. 13; Library of Congress/Wikimedia Commons, p. 27; National Anthropological Archives, Smithsonian Institution (ESC19.15), p. 19; National Museum of the American Indian, Smithsonian Institution, pp. 9 (P09358), 17 (P26733); Pat Bonish/Alamy Photo, p. 23; Sarah Quintans/Shutterstock Images, p. 5; Smithsonian American Art Museum, p. 25

Library of Congress Control Number: 2021943201

Publisher's Cataloging-in-Publication Data

Names: Bird, F.A., author.
Title: Comanche / by F.A. Bird
Description: Minneapolis, Minnesota : Abdo Publishing, 2022 | Series: Native American nations | Includes online resources and index.
Identifiers: ISBN 9781532197185 (lib. bdg.) | ISBN 9781098219314 (ebook)
Subjects: LCSH: Comanche Indians--Juvenile literature. | Indians of North America--Juvenile literature. | Indigenous peoples--Social life and customs--Juvenile literature. | Cultural anthropology--Juvenile literature.
Classification: DDC 973.0497--dc23

Contents

Homelands 4
Society 6
Homes 8
Food 10
Clothing 12
Crafts 14
Family 16
Children 18
Traditions 20
War 22
Contact with Europeans 24
Quanah Parker 26
The Comanche Today 28
Glossary 30
Online Resources 31
Index 32

CHAPTER 1

Homelands

The Comanche have lived in North America for thousands of years. For many centuries, the Comanche were part of the large Northern Shoshone tribe. They lived in the mountains of Wyoming and Colorado.

In the 1600s, the Comanche acquired horses from the Spanish, who had started exploring North America. The Comanche used these horses to travel to the plains of eastern Colorado and Kansas. There, they hunted buffalo.

The Comanche were fierce warriors and skilled horsemen. Soon, they pushed other tribes aside. They moved farther south into Oklahoma and Texas. The Comanche were most powerful in the early 1800s. The tribe had about 10,000 people.

The Wichita Mountains of Oklahoma are part of Comanche territory.

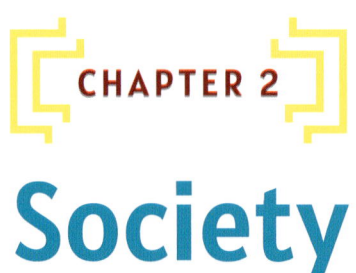

CHAPTER 2
Society

The Comanche tribe was made up of several large bands. A family could live with any Comanche band they chose. These Comanche bands all spoke the same language. They rarely fought with each other.

The Penateka, or "honey eaters," lived in central Texas. North of them lived the Nokoni, or "wanderers." The Kotsoteka, or "buffalo eaters," lived in Oklahoma. The Yamparika, or "root eaters," lived in Kansas. The Quahadi, or "antelope eaters," lived in west Texas and New Mexico.

Each band followed the advice of peace chiefs, who were respected **elders**. Peace chiefs were wise, even-tempered, and generous. They possessed great knowledge of the land. Peace chiefs from different family camps often met in **council**. They helped solve the band's problems.

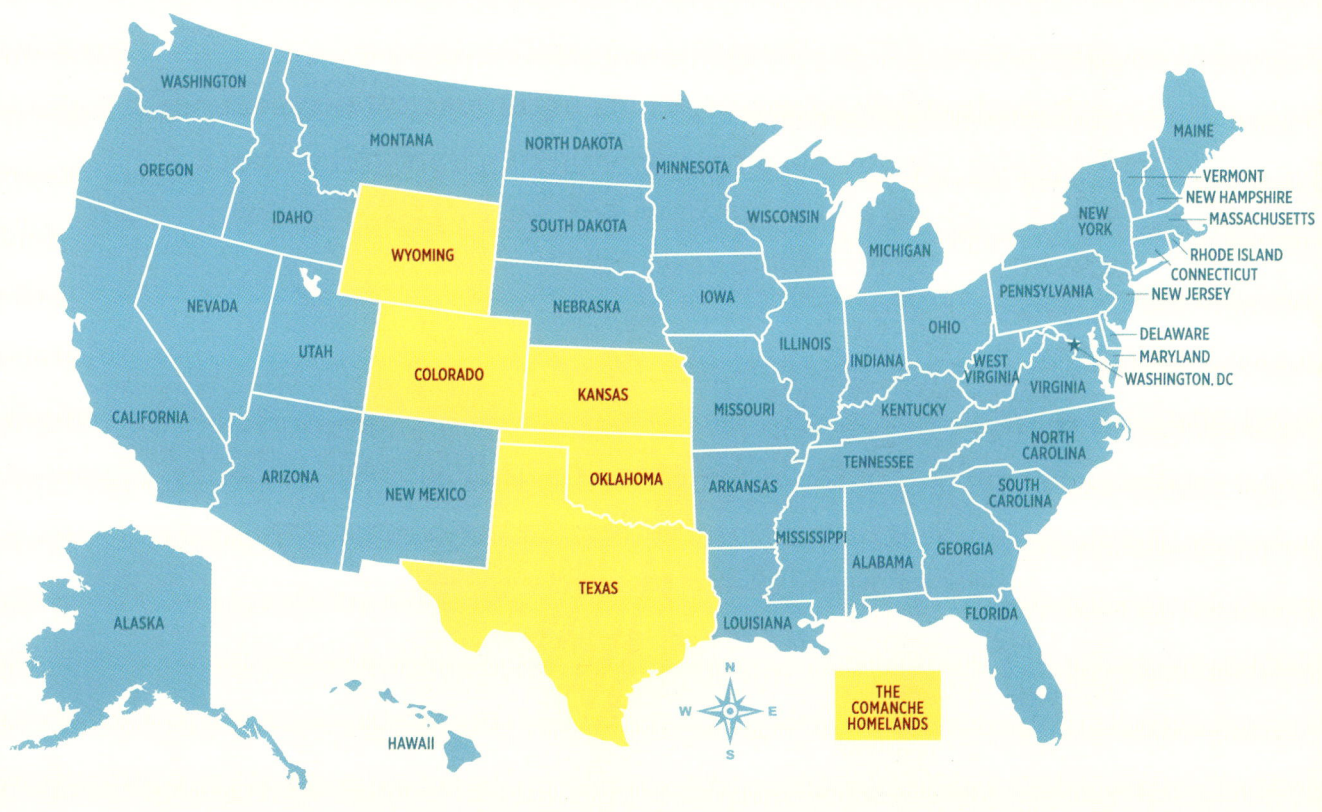

CHAPTER 3

Homes

The Comanche moved often in search of buffalo, pecans, prickly pears, and other food. So, they lived in tepees, which were easy to take down and move. The Comanche fitted their horses with a **travois**. It carried heavy loads, including tepees.

A tepee was about 15 feet (4.6 m) high. Its base was about 15 feet (4.6 m) across. In the summer, the buffalo hides near the base were rolled up. This allowed a cool breeze to pass through the tepee. In the winter, furs were piled on the ground inside the tepee. A fire was built in the center of the tepee. Flaps in the top of the tepee allowed smoke to escape.

The tepee frame was covered with buffalo hides. A Comanche woman could put up a tepee in about fifteen minutes.

Food

When they lived in Wyoming and Colorado, the Comanche were hunter-gatherers. They hunted deer and elk. They gathered foods that grew naturally.

When the Comanche moved to Kansas and eastern Colorado, most of their food and supplies came from buffalo. In the summer and fall, the entire **band** moved near the buffalo herds. Men on horseback surrounded a small herd. Then, they rode among the buffalo, shooting them with arrows.

Once a buffalo was killed, the men skinned it. They cut the meat and carried it back to camp. The women prepared the meat. They hung it on drying racks. Then, the women and girls prepared the buffalo hides for **tanning**.

The Comanche did not waste any part of the buffalo. Horns were made into ladles and cups. Sinew from the back of the buffalo was used for thread and bowstrings.

CHAPTER 5
Clothing

Comanche women often wore knee-length, deerskin skirts. They had **fringe** along the seams and hem. A **poncho**-like top was worn with the skirt. It was made from one animal skin and had a narrow opening for the wearer's head to go through.

Men wore knee-length **breechcloths**. They were decorated with shells and long fringe. Leggings were worn tied below the knees.

Young girls wore deerskin breechcloths. When they were around the age of 12, they wore buckskin dresses. Boys wore deerskin breechcloths throughout their lives.

In cold weather, the Comanche wore shirts made of deer, mountain sheep, or antelope hides. Men, women, and children wore buffalo robes in the coldest weather. Men also wore fur-lined leggings.

Comanche men wore their hair in long braids that they sometimes wrapped with fur or ribbons. They parted their hair in the middle.

CHAPTER 6

Crafts

Comanche men made bows and arrows. Most bows were made of strong, flexible wood from the Osage orange tree. The wood was cut and scraped to the right size. After drying for several months, the wood was greased with buffalo fat. Then it was wrapped with thin, wet strips of buffalo **tendon**. The tendon shrank as it dried, so it tightened around the wood.

Bowstrings were made from several strips of tendon. They were twisted and held together with glue. The Comanche made glue by boiling buffalo horns and hooves.

Making arrows required great skill. Each shaft had to be carefully crafted so the arrow could hit its target. Feathers were attached to one end of the shaft to make the arrow fly straight. An arrowhead was attached to the other end.

Comanche men crafted shields from buffalo hide. Sometimes they painted decorations on their shields' covers.

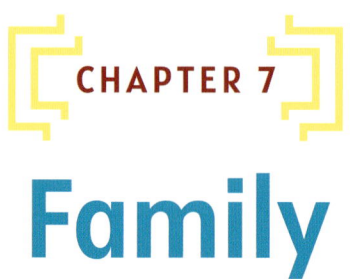

CHAPTER 7

Family

Before a Comanche man could get married, he had to complete a vision quest and take part in raids. Afterward, his family held a ceremony to honor him. Then, he could marry.

The man took a present of horses to the woman's family. If the family accepted the horses, and the man agreed to care for the woman's parents, the man and woman were married. Then, the woman moved into the man's tepee.

Comanche families had few children. The parents, older children, uncles, and aunts raised each child. Boys moved into their own tepees when they became teenagers. Girls remained with their parents until they married.

A Comanche mother and child

CHAPTER 8

Children

When Comanche babies were born, they were washed and bundled in soft furs. Moss was used as a diaper. The babies were placed on a **cradleboard** for protection.

Children could have many names before they were given their adult name. The father usually named the baby. But sometimes, a friend was asked to name it during a ceremony.

If Comanche children misbehaved, their parents told them stories. The stories were told in a way that made the children understand proper behavior, and what was expected of them.

The grandparents helped raise the children. They told their grandchildren stories. These stories taught them about the history and ways of their people. Children also learned by playing games that **imitated** adult roles.

A Comanche cradleboard was made of a leather basket. It held the baby onto the backboard. Another leather covering was placed over the woven basket and attached to the board.

Traditions

The Comanche believe the Great Spirit created them from the dust swirls of a mighty storm. After humans were created, Earth wondered how it was going to feed the people.

The Great Spirit thought about Earth's concern. The Great Spirit decided that Earth would feed humans physically during the day. At night, while they slept, the Great Spirit would feed them spiritually.

The Evil Spirit was cast out of the Spirit World after it refused to recognize humans as the Great Spirit's best creation. The Evil Spirit's punishment was to roam the earth forever.

The Evil Spirit caused sickness, death, and hardship for humans. Finally, the Great Spirit cast the Evil Spirit into a bottomless pit. But the spirit hid in the fangs and stingers of poisonous creatures.

The Comanche believe that the Evil Spirit continues to harm people through creatures such as the striped bark scorpion.

War

Warriors in a Comanche war party wore buffalo horns or eagle feathers tied in their hair. They were experts with the bow and arrow and rifle. Some warriors carried lances and buffalo-hide shields.

Not all warfare was violent. The Comanche also **counted coup**. Counting coup on one's enemy was dangerous, but it was considered rewarding. To count coup, a warrior had to touch an enemy warrior with a stick and then get safely away.

To be touched by one's enemy was an insult. It meant that the enemy could have easily killed you. The person counting coup was respected for being able to get close to his enemy without killing him.

Comanche warriors often painted their faces before battle.

Contact with Europeans

Early in the 1700s, a Ute trading party brought other Native Americans to the Spanish settlements in New Mexico. The Spanish asked for the name of the other Native Americans. The Utes called them *Koh-Mahts*. That word meant "those who want to fight us."

The Spaniards began to call these people *Komantcia*. Then American settlers called them Comanche. But the Comanche called themselves the *Numinu* or *Nemene*. It means "The People."

The Comanche traded hides for European guns, knives, glass beads, kettles, cloth, and blankets. The Comanche traded horses to other tribes for goods such as animal skins, tobacco, and tepee poles.

Horses let the Comanche move fast enough to hunt buffalo.

Quanah Parker

Quanah Parker was the last chief of the Quahadi band of Comanche. On June 27, 1874, Parker led 700 warriors in a fight with the US Army. It was called the Battle of Adobe Walls. Adobe Walls was a trading post and fort in Texas. American buffalo hunters used the fort as a place to trade buffalo hides.

The hunters threatened the buffalo herds. And they threatened the Native American way of life. The Comanche, Cheyenne, and Kiowa fought hard. But they were no match for the long-range rifles of the buffalo hunters.

Parker was the last of the Comanche war leaders to surrender to the US Army. He brought the Quahadi to the Indian **Reservation** in Oklahoma. Parker also served as a judge on the reservation's Court of Indian Offenses. These courts upheld US laws on reservations.

Parker became a spokesman for his people because he could speak Spanish, English, and Comanche.

CHAPTER 13
The Comanche Today

Today, the Comanche headquarters is near Lawton, Oklahoma. The tribe has about 15,000 members. About half of them live in the Lawton area. The Comanche are preserving their traditional ways by teaching their people the Comanche language.

There are Comanche **powwows** nearly every weekend somewhere in the United States. The biggest one is the Comanche Nation Homecoming Powwow. It is held each July in Walters, Oklahoma. Powwows include traditional drumming, dancing, food, and crafts.

Powwows give native and non-native communities the opportunity to share the rich history, traditions, and spirituality of the Comanche people. They also allow people to enjoy a spirit of friendship and community.

A Comanche dancer at the 2019 Comanche Nation Fair Powwow in Lawton, Oklahoma

Glossary

band—a number of persons acting together; a subgroup of a tribe.

breechcloth—a piece of cloth, usually worn by men. It wraps between the legs and around the waist.

council—a group of people who meet, usually to make decisions.

counting coup (KOUNT-ing KOO)—a military action where Comanche warriors touched the enemy without killing him, then returned safely to camp.

cradleboard—a decorated flat board with a wooden band at the top that protects the baby's head.

elder—a person having authority because of age or experience.

fringe—a border or trim made of threads or cords, either loose or tied together in small bunches.

imitate—to try to be like; to follow the example of.

poncho—a large piece of cloth or other material with a slit in the middle for the head to go through.

powwow—a ceremony of Native Americans, usually involving feasts, dancing, and performances.

raid—a sudden attack.

reservation—a piece of land set aside by the government for Native Americans to live on.

tan—to make a hide into leather by soaking it in a special liquid.

tendon—a band of tough fibers that joins a muscle to a bone. It is also called sinew.

travois (truh-VOI)—a frame of two wooden poles tied together over the back of an animal and allowed to drag on the ground. It was used to transport loads.

vision quest—a spiritual journey to witness the mystical or supernatural.

ONLINE RESOURCES

To learn more about the Comanche, please visit **abdobooklinks.com** or scan this QR code. These links are routinely monitored and updated to provide the most current information available.

Index

Adobe Walls, Battle of, 26
animals, 4, 6, 8, 10, 12, 14, 16, 20, 22, 24, 26
Army, US, 26

bands, 6, 10, 26

Cheyenne, 26
children, 12, 16, 18
clothes, 12
Colorado, 4, 10
counting coup, 22
Court of Indian Offenses, 26
cradleboards, 18

family, 6, 16, 18
food, 6, 8, 10, 28

hunting, 4, 10, 26

Kansas, 4, 6, 10
Kiowa, 26
Kotsoteka, 6

New Mexico, 6, 24
Nokoni, 6
North America, 4, 6, 10, 24, 26, 28
Northern Shoshone, 4

Oklahoma, 4, 6, 26, 28

Parker, Quanah, 26
peace chiefs, 6
Penateka, 6
powwows, 28

Quahadi, 6, 26

seasons, 8, 10, 12
settlers, 4, 24
Spain, 4, 24

tepees, 8, 16
Texas, 4, 6, 26
trading, 24, 26
traditions, 20, 28

United States, 4, 6, 10, 24, 26, 28
Ute, 24

vision quests, 16

war, 4, 16, 22, 26
weapons, 14, 22, 24
Wyoming, 4, 10

Yamparika, 6